T0197443

HEAVENLY VISIONS

a Gathering of Souls

CAROL J. CARVER

BALBOA.
PRESS

A DIVISION OF HAY HOUSE

Balboa Press books may be ordered through booksellers or by contacting:

Balboa Press
A Division of Hay House
1663 Liberty Drive
Bloomington, IN 47403
www.balboapress.com
1 (877) 407-4847

Because of the dynamic nature of the Internet, any web addresses or
links contained in this book may have changed since publication and
may no longer be valid. The views expressed in this work are solely those
of the author and do not necessarily reflect the views of the publisher,
and the publisher hereby disclaims any responsibility for them.

The author of this book does not dispense medical advice or prescribe the use
of any technique as a form of treatment for physical, emotional, or medical
problems without the advice of a physician, either directly or indirectly. The
intent of the author is only to offer information of a general nature to help
you in your quest for emotional and spiritual well-being. In the event you use
any of the information in this book for yourself, which is your constitutional
right, the author and the publisher assume no responsibility for your actions.

This book is a work of non-fiction. Unless otherwise noted, the author
and the publisher make no explicit guarantees as to the accuracy of
the information contained in this book and in some cases, names of
people and places have been altered to protect their privacy.

Scripture taken from the King James Version of the Bible.

Print information available on the last page.

ISBN: 978-1-5043-5348-9 (sc)
ISBN: 978-1-5043-5347-2 (e)

Library of Congress Control Number: 2016904257

Balboa Press rev. date: 3/30/2016

This book is dedicated to my loving husband, Floyd.

Thank you for being supportive of me as I have begun to fulfill this particular call of God on my life. You have been patient to let me get off alone and write into the wee hours of the night and even more patient as I have attempted to learn all that I can about writing, publishing and about computers. You know that has been no easy tasks for me! You recognize it as the calling that it is and have encouraged me in every way imaginable to begin it. Thank you for taking this journey with me. I appreciate you more than you may realize.

And as with each and every book that I write, this book is also dedicated to my Heavenly Father, who has loved me, encouraged me and been kind enough to show me great and marvelous things of what is in store for those who have put their hope and trust in His son. And to His son Jesus Christ, my loving Savior, my eternal thanks. You gave your life so that we might have eternal life in Heaven. My prayer for this book is that people see the love that you have for them and come to know you in a more personal way.

And many thanks…

To my good friend Lisa Kennan for her help in typing and editing this book. You asked me many questions and helped me to clarify some of my writing. My eternal gratitude for answering my many computer questions so patiently and bringing me into the 21ˢᵗ century. You know you're not done answering them, right? I know we both count it as a true blessing from God when we were introduced all those years ago. We've been friends for a long time and I count you as one of my dearest.

Many thanks to Robert Colon for his wise counsel and direction; and to the entire team at Balboa Press. What a grand adventure you have begun me on! You and your entire team have been such a joy to work with. Thanks for bringing me along and being so patient with my numerous questions about the strange world of self-publishing. Thanks for all your help and encouragement!

INTRODUCTION

This book is a recounting of the several times that I have been allowed to see Heaven. I never physically (with my actual body) went there, that I know of at any rate, although it sure felt like it at the time. Although I was raised in the Christian faith, I didn't come to an understanding about supernatural signs and wonders that the Bible talks about until I was in my early twenties. Up until then, I knew about God, but didn't "know" Him. I hadn't made a personal commitment to Him and accepted the salvation that He offered. I had a little understanding that God was as real in our lives as we wanted Him to be simply by watching my parents, but I didn't know much. I didn't understand then that God wants to be very active in people's lives and display "signs and wonders" for all believers, but many believers don't ask Him to. In other words, I believe in God and His supernatural power and manifestations. At the age of nineteen I had a personal relationship with Jesus Christ and had accepted Him into my heart as both my Savior and my Lord. My dad, also a Christian, had told me that I had "a calling" on my life, but I didn't understand what that meant back then.

Over many years, as God began to teach me His Word and His ways, I began to have an understanding about the power of God and how it can manifest in the lives of those who believe on Him. In my opinion, I'm just an ordinary person and not someone "special", except that I am extremely curious about things. People have asked me over the years why I was allowed to visit Heaven so many times and my simple answer is, "because I asked to!" When I was allowed to see Heaven I wasn't afraid, but I felt a wonderful peace and so much love that I didn't want to come back to earth. Of all the angels I've seen, none of them told me their names. And believe me, I asked them!

Every time I saw an angel, I always saw a brilliant white light surrounding him. I say him because every angel I saw looked masculine, tall and handsome. Some had wings and some did not. They were soft spoken, but they spoke with an authoritative voice.

Some people are afraid of death for themselves or for their loves ones that they have lost. My purpose of this book is to share God's love, His Word, and what He has prepared for you. I wanted to see Heaven to have the knowledge for myself and to be able to tell the truth about it to others, especially to comfort those who had lost someone in death. It really isn't about me, but it's about God and His son, Jesus Christ. I want to obey Him because He has done so much for me. All the glory belongs to Him. If it weren't for God, I couldn't have seen Heavenly things or heard what I was told.

I'm also sharing part of my life and what God allowed me to see to tell you that there is no fear in death when you have accepted Jesus Christ into your heart. Heaven is a real place, a place where you will feel tremendous love and peace. In death you will never go alone. An angel will escort you to Heaven.

After I shared what I saw about Heaven, angels, and seeing Jesus Christ, I have received a lot of persecution because people do not believe me. I'm not here to change their minds about it, and I don't try. These experiences have brought me closer to Jesus Christ and to God the Father. I will never change what I have seen because it is the truth. Since some people here on earth are named Jesus, I will always say Jesus Christ so that you can distinguish the difference.

A Sense Of Humor

God is a creator. Do you realize that one of the many things He created was laughter and that He has a sense of humor? God Himself laughs! Trust me, he does. (Psalm 37:13) I'll share a personal story with you. I think that this story will illustrate a lot about me and God.

My dad loved the Lord and talked to Him every day. Only having one hand, he depended on God for everything to make him independent. He worked a full time job, raised eight children, painted, trained show horses, washed dishes before we had a dishwasher, swept floors, did carpentry work (with some help), had a first class Engineer's License, and still found time to minister to everyone he could that would listen. He had a lot of spiritual gifts, like discernment, knowledge, wisdom and those gifts enabled him to love people and witness to them, as well as have dreams and visions.

My dad and I talked a lot. One day he was very serious in wanting to tell me something important. "Carol," he said, "the day will come when I won't be here to tell you things from God. You will receive my mantle. Use it wisely." He didn't tell me what that meant. I was young and didn't know very much about the Bible at that time. I knew mostly about salvation and The Lord's Prayer and the Ten Commandments—but not much else.

We had a living room with a fireplace. Above it was a wooden mantle. I wondered why dad would want me to have that wooden mantle. How would I disconnect it? And it wouldn't look right being gone with all the marble around it. What in the world would I replace it with? I didn't ask dad about it because sometimes when I asked him things he would tell me to pray and that God would reveal it to me.

Years passed, and I still thought the mantle that I was to receive was on that living room fireplace. I'd look at it and wonder why it was so special. My dad had died and I was married with children. We were living in that home along with my mother. One of my sons could do carpentry work. I asked him how I'd ever get that mantle off of the wall. He said, "You don't want to take it off. It would ruin the looks of it." He didn't understand that my dad wanted me to have it (or so I believed at the time), but I wouldn't tell him. God must have had a good chuckle about this misunderstanding.

I felt the call of God into ministry. I read the Bible for myself and I read it all the time. I finally read about Elijah and Elisha. Elisha wanted Elijah's mantle when he went to heaven. Oh my goodness! That is what my dad had tried to tell me! Not knowing, I didn't understand because I was ignorant of God's Word. Thank God I was learning.

Now you know why I think God has a sense of humor. It was the anointing and calling of God on his life, being transferred to my life, that dad tried to tell me about. When I tell people about it today, I can laugh with God because I believe it's funny. I can imagine God telling my dad about what a time He had getting me to understand about "the mantle" And I'm pretty sure that they both had a good chuckle about how long it took me to get that concept.

I imagine hearing my dad say, "Finally!" If God is telling you something you don't understand, don't quit. Keep going and keep praying and reading God's Bible, and you will understand, too.

MINISTRY

I knew I had a ministry for God to do. I wasn't sure I would want to do it because He had me do some hard things before. Ministering to people isn't always easy.

During this time I went to several churches, always sitting in the last pew so I wouldn't be noticed. Many times the pastor of the church would pick me out of the crowd and tell me God was going to send me to the hurting, the suffering and the abused. I would always ask, "Where?" and each one would say that God will tell you. Everything that you are learning you will be able to share. You are in training.

In fulfilling that call, God had me to visit people in jails and prisons. I was faithful to that calling for twenty-five years before God released me from it. I told them about

Jesus Christ. I didn't visit them as a judge but as a child of God. I told them that their past wasn't the important thing, but where they would spend their future for eternity was what was important.

I was taken to Heaven several times and each time I was taken there by a different angel. I always felt such a peace being with the angel because I knew he was sent by God to take me to heaven. We arrived on the outside of the city of Heaven. I could see the open gate ahead of us. In front of me was a burning bush. I fell to the ground on my face and said, "Forgive me, Jesus Christ," over and over. "I want to come to this place to stay forever."

Jesus Christ was standing in front of me. I looked into his brown eyes and face and felt such love. He picked me up with His hands, looked me in my eyes and said, "I've already forgiven you. You don't have to beg." The more I looked at his eyes, the more love I felt.

His brown hair was one layer that came to the bottom of his hairline on His neck. It wasn't long like the pictures try to portray Him. He had a long white robe that reached to his feet. A gold braided belt was around His waist and hung down. He had brown sandals on His feet. A purple sash was from His shoulder to the other side of His waist. I don't know what He called it.

I said, "So I'll know the truth, where are the scars on your hands and wrists?"

He showed me His hands, wrists, and feet. They weren't scars, but holes!

"Oh, I didn't realize all the pain you went through. I love you", I said. And then He was gone.

THE MOVE

I was visiting a church. While I was there, a couple asked me to go over to their house and share my testimony with them. They wanted to share their testimony with me as well.

We went to their house and I remarked how beautiful I thought it was. I asked him if he would share his testimony first. He was the Associate Pastor. He shared how his wife wanted their dream house, but that they didn't see how they would ever get it, so they remodeled their house. They would be content to live there forever. When the last window was put in, God told them to look for their "dream house".

She knew of a house she wanted and when they went to look at it, it was for sale. God worked it out so that they could afford it. This was the very house I was sitting in! I thought to myself, I am remodeling my house which my mother had given to me once she had her stroke. The last thing I was having done was the windows. As a matter of fact, I only had one window to go, just like they did! But, I thought the testimony was for them and not for me. I wondered why he felt that he had to share that particular testimony with me.

Time went by and the last window was completed in my house. While I was praying one day, the Lord spoke to me to sell the house because I was moving. So, I asked the Lord, "Where?"

"To be with your daughter and granddaughter," He replied.

"Jonah", I cried, "I can identify with you! I don't want to go!" I was self-employed and loved my church, friends, all of the flowers in my yard and having so much family near to me. When I didn't act on what He had told me to do right away, I realized that my family and friends stopped coming by very often. My customers would call me to say that they didn't need me anymore for different reasons.

How would I move all of our belongings from the Midwest to several states away? God finally had my attention on the matter. I needed a vacation so I could be alone to think. My daughter called and asked for my mom and I to come visit them and look over the town. She could even get me a job if I decided to stay. I told her I would pray about it and for her to call me back. Before I knew it, plans were made for her to come and get us. We would go for the visit, but I wasn't staying. I didn't want to hurt her feelings or disobey God, but I really didn't want to pick up and move. Maybe I had heard wrong. I'd pray again.

We went and looked around. It was nice, but not home. More prayer was needed. God said to move there. I really didn't think my mom would ever agree. For seventy-nine years she had lived in the same state. So I asked her and she said, "How soon can you put the house up for sale?" I could have fallen off my chair!

A dear Christian friend and a Pastor gave me the name of the very same Christian realtor who had assisted that Associate Pastor and his wife at that church I had visited to find their dream home. The house went up for sale. We had yard sales and gave several things away to churches that had a mission. We packed (and packed) our remaining things.

Although we were preparing physically for our move, I needed to begin to prepare mentally. Memories and the way we deal with them depend on our attitude. You can't run or hide from them. You take them with you. I can take all the good memories from all these years in this area of the country with me when I go and I can cherish them anywhere. And I can decide to welcome the new challenge that this new location will bring, I decided. I certainly didn't want to be knowingly disobedient to what I felt God was telling me to do. We can be disobedient in our actions but we can also physically do what has been asked of us, but have a rotten attitude. I decided that God had helped us make it back to the Midwest from our vacation and with God we will make it here to start a new home. We are Overcomers by Jesus' blood. Praise God! I still had too many possessions so I gave some more away and sold some. It's comforting to know that Jesus Christ is everywhere, not just in one place.

Fear of the unknown of anything is an attitude. I understand the scripture "Perfect love casteth out fear" (see I John 4:18a KJV). When I asked my mom why she hadn't told me we were supposed to move, she simply said, "You never asked me." When I shared with her what God had told me, she said, "I know. God already told me. I was just waiting for Him to tell you."

That was a miracle in itself. Mom had lived in the same house for fifty-three years. To pack up and move was not a problem for her because she knew God had spoken to her.

I was glad I had obeyed God because the house we moved to was a lot smaller and I realized we didn't need all of the possessions we had accumulated. I still had more than what I needed. The Lord told me not to hoard things, but to go through them and give away everything He told me I didn't need. I had so many things I wasn't using and had in storage in case I ever needed them. Hoarding is beyond an attitude. It is selfishness.

When I had a ministry, people gave me clothes that had holes, were blood-stained, or very dirty, which I threw away. I always gave people the best things I had to make them happy. I only gave away what I would like to receive. As I prayed and asked God who I should give things to, I was introduced to a lady that was starting a ministry like I had before I moved here. I knew God was changing my direction. It didn't surprise me that she needed all the possessions that I had to give away.

She had a house and was going to help abused women have a place to stay. I knew how to pray for them because it is what I had been doing for years. As I already mentioned, it isn't always easy to minister to people. I knew she would have a lot of problems ahead of her, but with God's help, she could do it.

And God had helped us find a house that wasn't too far away from my daughter and granddaughters. We really enjoyed being nearer to them.

Restoration Of Our Family

I found a church I liked and had met some of the people. I decided that God knew what He was doing and I would adjust in this new state after all. I apologized to God for all of the questions and doubts that I had before I came here. I have always loved to write but I didn't think I would ever be an author until God told me to write about my experiences once I had moved to North Carolina.

He taught me a lot through ministering to so many different kinds of people, my marriage, divorce and re-marriage. When I didn't like something with my husband, I would go to God and ask Him to change my husband. But God would always change my attitude first. When I was praying, God would tell me to buy my husband a gift, talk to him, go places with him that he liked to go, and to let him know he was special to me. When I obeyed God, my husband's attitude would change towards me. The Lord would add things like, "Be a good listener and work in the garden with him." Communication is very important. Just like God desires to talk with us, so should we be able to talk to one another. There are so many sources of education today. We don't need to be boring. Life can be exciting, and I believe people need that. They will want to be around you if you are positive.

Over a span of many years, several things happened to my husband. He was called by God to preach but he said it was too hard for him to live it. He didn't want to disgrace God by not being able to live a consistent Christian lifestyle and eventually he backslid. He became bitter over how some people treated him and he had unforgiveness towards them. To ease his guilt over not obeying the call to preach, he drank alcohol. If you don't drink alcohol, which I didn't, it's very hard to live with someone that does and to be the Christian that God wants you to be. To be honest, I fought having resentment and unforgiveness myself, but I'd pray and read my Bible to overcome it. God was always faithful.

Years passed and my husband became sick. The doctor told him that he had cancer. He had 3 surgeries and chemotherapy and he really suffered. Early one morning the Lord told me to ask him what he would do if God gave him a complete miracle. He didn't answer me, but hung his head down and looked sad. I knew he was refusing it because he wanted to go to Heaven now. I wanted him to have a miracle and prayed for it. I was so disappointed that he didn't receive it. After that, he lost weight and couldn't eat. The chemo treatments were hard on him and he knew that he was going to die.

I called to tell his family that he wanted to see them before he died. They lived out of state. They came to see him and were able to visit with him. He wanted to talk to his mom in private so everyone left them alone to talk. One by one he had told everyone that he had accepted Christ back into his heart and prayed all the time. He gave his testimony to anyone that would listen. In the meantime, I thought back to when he had all his surgeries. I was all by myself. Everywhere I looked, there were people together waiting for their loved ones. I told God I didn't like to be alone in such a crisis and was wondering how I was going to make it when he passed on and went to Heaven. Our daughter and I were with him at the hospital when he died. I was disappointed that I didn't see an angel come for him or hear heavenly music. God had me to try to comfort our daughter. We tried to take care of each other during that time.

The week after he died, people from the churches we attended came to see us with their love, prayers, food and fellowship. I told God He didn't forget my prayer back when he had surgery and I felt alone. God gave me such peace and comfort in those weeks after he died. What a blessing!

Things settled down and time passed, when I received a phone call from his mom. She wanted to tell me about their conversation when they were alone before he died. He had asked her not to tell me until after he was gone. He said he knew I wanted him to have a miracle, but it wasn't going to happen. He chose to go to heaven now. His chance for ministry was over and his time was up. At least he knew Christ had forgiven him. He wanted to see God and our two children who weren't here on earth. He also wanted her to tell me that he loved them but it was too painful for him to talk about. Lastly, he wanted for me to forgive him for the wrong things he had done.

When we married the first time, we had lost two children through miscarriages. He didn't talk to me about it. Ever. I felt hurt. When his mother told me this, I felt a release of the hurt I had for forty-six years of wondering why he didn't tell me about his feelings of our lost children. God is so good to take away all of our hurts. He cares for us so much!

So you can understand a little better, let me tell you that I met my first husband when we were sophomores in high school. I was just 15 at the time. We dated off and on for five years before we got married. We were both nineteen then. To me, I thought he was a handsome guy. I said all this to explain that the chemotherapy that he took make his teeth look rotten; he was thin; he lost a lot of weight, strength and joy. He suffered so much. He was in a hospital bed in our living room so that I could take care of him. He finally had to go to the hospital, where he was only there for a day and an evening, before he died.

The day after he died, I had taken a shower and was leaving the bathroom. I reached up to turn off the light when I saw my husband surrounded by a brilliant white light. He was wearing a white robe; he was smiling at me with a healthy, young body. He was sixty-six years old when he died, but at that moment he looked like he did back when we started dating.

I need to jump back a little further to explain some more. My husband and I had been divorced for several years. I was still living in the Midwest with my mother at that time, and he had moved to North Carolina. He had a good job as a supervisor and he seemed to like the weather in North Carolina most of all. God sometimes works in ways that we don't understand. It takes time to reveal His plan for us. I certainly didn't see this one coming!

Well, once we moved there I didn't know anyone and I still didn't have a job -- and boy, did I ever need one. My ex-husband offered me a job and I took it. It was the hardest job I ever had in my life. The work was physically demanding and it was very hard for me to have my ex-husband as my supervisor. We had to talk to each other every day. That was a start. Eventually, after work he asked me to go out on a date, which I accepted. Time passed and on our original wedding date we decided to remarry. It was amazing how we could forgive, love and trust each other again.

LOSING BABIES

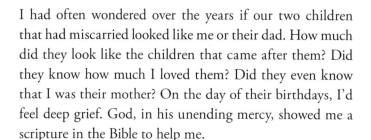

I had often wondered over the years if our two children that had miscarried looked like me or their dad. How much did they look like the children that came after them? Did they know how much I loved them? Did they even know that I was their mother? On the day of their birthdays, I'd feel deep grief. God, in his unending mercy, showed me a scripture in the Bible to help me.

John 14:1-3 (KJV)

> *1Let not your heart be troubled: ye believe in God, believe also in me. 2In my Father's house are many mansions: if it were not so, I would have told you. I go to prepare a place for you. 3And if I go and prepare a place for*

> *you, I will come again, and receive you unto*
> *myself; that where I am, there ye may be also.*

As soon as I read these scriptures, my living room filled with a light so bright that I could hardly see. God told me that He'd allowed me to see Heaven so that I could write a book and tell people what I'd seen. Heaven is such an interesting place!

An angel stood before me dressed in a brilliant white robe. At a rapid speed we flew through the atmosphere. I wasn't afraid because the angel held me with one of his arms.

He looked handsome, about seven feet tall and masculine to me. He seemed powerful with his magnificent wings outstretched. I felt very safe because I knew God had sent him. As we approached the entrance, the iridescent Gate of Pearl was so bright that I knew God had to adjust my eyes so I could see. I believed Heaven was all white, but to my amazement, I saw colors everywhere. They were incredibly vivid and beautiful. All of God's angels are beautiful, but they aren't all the same size nor do they look exactly alike. God has an organization to everything. God's angels have strength to do what we cannot do.

Outside the entrance was the prettiest green grass I'd ever seen. Each blade of grass seemed alive and vivid with color as I looked at it. It didn't seem to show any footprints, nor did it look worn where people had walked on it before. Flowers were also vivid with colors I had never seen before so I cannot describe them. Each and every color was more vibrant than our eyes can see or our minds can register. Their fragrances were all different but blended together in a beautiful aroma. They stood so tall where they were planted and with the exceptionally bright colors; they looked so lively looking that I thought they could talk to me but they didn't. Everything was perfect with nothing out of place. I felt so much joy, peace and happiness. No dust or pollution anywhere. I could breathe so easy there.

Standing on the grass, I saw my dad that had gone to Heaven several years ago. While he'd been on earth he had lost his right arm in a factory where he had worked before I was born. I had never seen his right arm, only an artificial arm that the doctors had made for him and he did almost everything with his "good" arm, his left hand. As I watched my dad, he threw a white ball with his *right* hand to some younger people. I saw his whole arm and hand, including his fingernails. The young boy and girl that were playing catch with my dad smiled at me. In heaven, there is a "knowing" about some things. Words don't have to be spoken because you just know certain things. I knew that these two children were the ones that I had lost in miscarriage; and somehow I also knew that they lived with my dad. They were no longer babies and looked so healthy and happy. I felt so excited! A scripture came to my mind:

Revelation 21:3-4 (KJV)

3And I heard a great voice out of heaven saying, Behold, the tabernacle of God is with men, and he will dwell with them, and they shall be his people, and God himself shall be with them, and be their God. 4And God shall wipe away all tears from their eyes; and there shall be no more death, neither sorrow, nor

> *crying, neither shall there be any more pain:*
> *for the former things are passed away.*

Oh, how I wanted to stay in such a wonderful place where love was everywhere. I could see and feel it. I told the angel I wanted to stay there forever. I never knew the angel's name, although I had asked. The angel told me I had to return to my home. I remember feeling very disappointed but the angel held on to me as we flew down the atmosphere and I was back at my house in the living room. The angel disappeared before my eyes. I wanted so badly to go back to heaven with him, but I wasn't allowed.

All the years I had carried the grief of not being able to raise those two children left me. They had known and loved me. They were waiting for me. They lived with my dad (their grandpa). That made it more special to me. They were safe in Heaven with my dad.

Psalm 139:14

> *I will praise thee; for I am fearfully and*
> *wonderfully made: marvelous are thy works;*
> *and that my soul knoweth right well.*

I praise God for a better, perfect place to go when we leave here. I've read different people's books on their experiences of seeing Heaven and a lot are different than what I saw. I believe that God uses each of our unique experiences that we have been through to communicate with us so that we will understand things better. And since Heaven is such a big place, there is no way that one person can see it all, but He shows different people different aspects of what is there. The Bible tells us to try the spirits and see if it all lines up with God's word (see I John 4:1). God never contradicts His word. Man is changing God's word, not God. Why would a perfect God need to change His perfect word? It's only because man doesn't want to obey a Holy God and changes the word of God to suit themselves.

Isaiah 61:10 (KJV)

I will greatly rejoice in the LORD, my soul shall be joyful in my God; for he hath clothed me with the garments of salvation, he hath covered me with the robe of righteousness, as a bridegroom decketh himself with ornaments, and as a bride adorneth herself with her jewels.

Knowing what it felt like to be devastated having two miscarriages, I began to share with women about my experience of losing my own children. They would ask me questions that I couldn't answer. To be able to minister to them more effectively, I prayed and asked Father God to show me Heaven and to give me answers so that the grief of these women could be healed in their emotions. I knew the heartbreak of losing a child and wanted to bring healing to those who had gone through the same thing.

The Nursery Of The Babies

The feeling of wanting to be in Heaven never fully left me. It wasn't always as strong, but I longed to be there. God allowed some time to pass before He sent another angel to take me to Heaven again. The angels didn't tell me their names (even though I always asked them), but they knew my name.

This particular angel said, "Carol, God has something He'd like to show you. It will surprise you." We rapidly flew through the atmosphere and were at the entrance of Heaven. I wanted to see the shape of the gate, but it was so bright, I couldn't tell. It was open and angels were there. I saw the start of a gold street made of pure gold. We began to fly somewhere and we entered a very large room that was awesome to see. It had a white ceiling with white walls with murals of rainbows and children playing covering those walls. It was a cheerful place with flowers of all kinds and colors. The floor looked like it was white marble, but not like the white marble that you and I have ever seen. It was brighter and it was all one piece! There weren't any cracks or even any grout to disrupt the whiteness of the floor.

Baby bassinets were lined up in row after row. There were ruffles on the bassinets in blue, green, pink and yellow. It was not only the most colorful room I had ever seen in my life, but it was the most beautiful.

Babies were awake and alert, happy and smiling. They were all dressed in white robes with different colors of trim for a boy or a girl. The robes were elegant. All of these babies were loved by God, Jesus Christ, the angels, any family that they had there, and all the ones in Heaven. All of them were well, beautiful and intelligent. They have wisdom given to them from God. They were perfect babies in every way. They all looked different from each other, just like here on earth, and they were all adorable.

I wanted to hold each one but I wasn't allowed. I knew I was there to observe. If the baby didn't have a name when then they were in earth's realm, then God Himself gave them a name that He liked. Think about that. For every child that, for whatever reason, hadn't been given a name, whether they had actually been born or not, God Himself named them. If the parent had given them a name, the baby kept that name. This room was huge and there were all the babies of miscarriages, abortions, and any other tragic event that had taken their young lives. Every one of them came to this nursery.

The angel told me the first face a baby saw was Jesus Christ's, then the angels. Next were their family members that had already entered into Heaven. They all helped to raise these babies. God loves them all so much. He talks to them.

As I looked around I saw a colorful rocking chair beside each bassinet. Babies were being held, rocked, talked to and sung to.

There were no germs of any kind. It's hard to explain, but it is a place of joy where you feel tremendous love. There isn't any sadness anywhere, but just like a celebration, lots of laughter. I could see that the babies were so happy being there.

They don't stay babies. They are a spirit but they grow. As they grow, they have different rooms to live in; they don't always stay babies in the nursery.

It was such a wonderfully comforting thought to realize that when my own two children had died before birth, that they were received in Heaven in this nursery full of love and laughter and that they were so well taken care of by everyone. Every single baby, no matter the circumstance that brought them there, are too.

REWARDS

There is a story in the Bible where Jesus healed ten lepers but only one came back to thank Him. Curious, I asked Jesus if it was always that way. It certainly seemed to be that way in my own life. Whether I was simply giving someone something or helping them to receive a miracle, more times than not they didn't even offer a simple thanks most of the time. I had wondered at this over the years, and finally one day it occurred to me to ask the Lord.

Immediately an angel took me to Heaven and I looked at the street. It was all gold. It was real gold, just like in my previous vision. I looked on the street and saw someone with their back to me who was talking to a little boy that looked like he was about eight years old. I wasn't able to hear their conversation.

While I was watching, the little boy came skipping happily to where I was standing. He looked up at me and I smiled at him.

"I was just talking with Jesus Christ, and He told me I'm in Heaven because of your prayers, so I just wanted to thank you." Then he happily skipped past me. I stood there amazed and looking all around. I didn't personally know this boy because I certainly didn't recognize him. But I "knew" that he was someone that somebody else had asked me to pray for. As I continued to look around, I saw the face of the one he had been talking to. He had turned around so I could see Him and He smiled at me. It was Jesus Christ.

You won't receive all of your "thank yous" on earth. That is one of your rewards when you come to Heaven. God cares, and a Book of Remembrance is being written about the ones that love Him.

Malachi 3:16 (KJV)

> *Then they that feared the Lord spoke often one to another: and the Lord harkened, and heard it, and a book of remembrance was written before him for them that feared the Lord, and that thought upon his name.*

Will God be pleased with the words that are written in your Book of Remembrance? Live in grace. Walk in faith. Are you living your life the way that you want your life to be written about for all eternity?

Children Love You

The children grow up and babies don't stay babies, but they never get old or look old. Jesus Christ told me that all the children desire for their parents to be saved and be in Heaven with them. Christ always tells them the truth. Every child is full of love and forgiveness. Anything that was done to them on earth, they forgive. They await their parents with open arms. Jesus Christ loves families and His desire is for you to be together. As He forgave us, He is the perfect one to teach about forgiveness, whether that is forgiving others or forgiving ourselves.

I was told there are many reasons why women miscarry. I didn't see God, but I did hear His voice. Some babies are too perfect to stay in this world, but they have to be conceived before they can enter into Heaven. They love you so much and they want to see you and be with you. If any parents read this and feel guilt, you need to know that all you have to do is ask Jesus Christ to forgive you. You will feel His peace. The Bible tells us that we all come short of the glory of God (see Romans 3:23). Then you forgive yourself. Another scripture tells us about being free from condemnation, which is an important aspect to remember while on the path to forgiving ourselves.

Romans 8:1-2 (KJV)

> **1** *There is* therefore now no condemnation to them which are in Christ Jesus, who walk not after the flesh, but after the Spirit. **2**For the law of the Spirit of life in Christ Jesus hath made me free from the law of sin and death.

We have a better home to go to and will be loved as we love each other. It's hard to picture a world with all love, isn't it? Everything in Heaven is all about love and is felt so strongly that excitement is everywhere. There isn't any boredom there. Everyone desires to serve God and others, including the children. You will always see a smile on their faces radiating with joy and love.

Ladies, if you have had a miscarriage, abortion or lost a child in any way, my prayer is that this will help you and you will have peace.

MY DAUGHTER

Situations arise in our lives that we aren't always happy about. One arrived in my life and I allowed myself to be depressed instead of praising God through the circumstance. As a matter of fact, I was complaining to God. I'm ashamed to admit it, but it's true.

It was early in the morning, and I was sitting on the couch. All of a sudden I heard, "Mother." I looked up toward the ceiling. It was so bright at first that I could hardly see. In the center of the brightness was my beautiful daughter that I had miscarried all those years before, and she was wearing a gorgeous white robe. "Why are you so sad? Christ doesn't want you to be sad."

"You're right. I love you," I replied, and she was gone. I experienced such a joy and peace that it seemed to fill my soul. I started praising God. All of the depression left me. I apologized to God.

I thought about what I had just seen. My daughter looked like a young teenager. She was so happy. She knew that I loved her. I was glad she knew I was her mother. God amazes me how He works out every detail. Do we realize how much He loves one individual? My daughter had long, wavy blonde hair. She was thin like I was at her age. She was perfect and wonderfully made, just like all of the others in Heaven.

The Little Girl With Tremendous Fear

A woman came to see me once. She had a very young daughter that had so much fear that she didn't want to go outside of their house. She asked me to go see her daughter. This young girl didn't talk to anyone if she didn't know them. I prayed and then I went to see her. This little one began talking to me as soon as I entered their house. She came over and sat on my lap as I sat in the kitchen chair. Her mother was astonished! As I was talking to this girl, I asked her why she was so afraid. She told me that she didn't know; she just was. I believed her.

She wanted to show me her beautiful bedroom. I called her by her name and told her that she wouldn't be afraid anymore. I walked into her room and immediately knew that there was a spirit of fear residing here. I could see fear just wash over her face, too. I rebuked the spirit in the name of Jesus Christ and commanded it to leave. Immediately, I saw a little cherub. I told her it would be with her all the time. She looked around and she saw it, too. It went and sat on her shoulder. I went back into the kitchen and talked to her mother and told her what I had seen. Her mother didn't know what to think, I'm sure.

After a time, the mother called me. "Praise God! I believe you now! My little girl isn't the same. She talks, goes outside to play, goes with me places, and has quit seeing her psychiatrist. She knows God is real and wants to go to church again. The angel talks to her. She knows he is there to protect her. She doesn't see him all the time, but she knows that he is there. Thank you, and Praise God!"

Yes, this happened on earth, but God sent her His angel from Heaven. I felt led to write this. God is no respecter of persons. Maybe you need His help. Pray and ask God to send His special angel to you or your loved one. The little girl is a grown woman now, but she never forgot the experience, nor did I.

THE ROBES

I was visiting at a church while they were having revival services and the pastor asked if anyone had a prayer request. At the back of the church, a little gray-haired lady stood up with tears streaming down her face.

"Pray for all of my children. They are all lost" and then she sat back down.

The second night of the revival, the pastor asked for prayer requests. The same little gray-haired lady, with tears streaming down her cheeks, requested prayer for her unsaved children again. As a congregation, we prayed for them to be committed and to fulfill their call to Jesus Christ. She sat back down.

Now it was the third night of the revival and the pastor asked for prayer requests. Again, with tears flowing, the same lady stood up and requested prayer for all of her unsaved children. The congregation prayed that when they were saved they would not backslide.

The Evangelist was going to pray for people. I wanted an answer from God, so I walked up to the front of the church. I felt an anointing of God just as the Associate Pastor came over to me. "God's anointed you for a purpose. Let God have His way", he said. I went under the power of God and fell backwards. I hit my head on the pew behind me with a thud, but it didn't hurt me a bit.

Immediately, I was in Heaven in a room full of excitement. I was excited, too, but didn't know why. It was a busy place. Angels and saints were talking to each other while moving all around the room.

I stopped an angel and asked, "What is going on here? Why is there such an excitement?"

"This is the room where the robes are made for all the saints that will be in Heaven", was his reply.

He talked with such joy. I looked closer because of the brilliant light all around. I saw sewing machines that I've never seen the likes of here on earth. Huge machines that put articulate designs on the robes. The materials for all the robes are different, but I don't have any idea what we have on earth to compare them to.

Angels were carrying tiny baby robes to adult robes. I don't know where they were kept, but each robe had a name tag on it awaiting the arrival of those that belong to Jesus Christ. The tags will be taken off when the saints arrive. Angels tell those sewing the robes how to make them; details such as colors, trim, flowers or whatever God tells them. The making of our robes are part of the rewards from the records that are kept in God's filing cabinets. Talents that we have that God gave us are used in Heaven also. I was surprised to see the huge sewing machines that could make so many different designs. You won't see any dust or hear any distracting or annoying types of noises in Heaven; only praises to God can be heard around the throne of God. By the way, Alleluia is always said with an A, not an H. Man has changed it because the devil wanted it to sound like Halloween.

Everything is organized and God is in control of every aspect of Heaven. I know I've said it before, but it bears repeating: Heaven is beautiful! It is so clean and colorful with all the flowers and jewels and streets of gold. An angel told me that God invented colors to be enjoyed. While I was there, another angel came up to me. He looked eight feet tall and he was carrying something. "God wants you to see this." I looked in his hands and saw a book. It was all white, very thick, and with parchment paper and real gold writing and there were numbers on the pages. The book was facing him. "This is the Lamb's Book of Life. Tell the little gray-haired lady at the back of the church to quit begging God for her unsaved children to accept Christ. Quit crying and believe God. You don't have to beg God. Ask, believe and receive. God knows the page her children's names will be written on. He knows what numbers would be on the page. The more she'd believe and praise Him, the sooner it would happen. Go back and tell her."

I was still on the floor at the church, coming out of seeing the vision. The Associate Pastor came over to me and said, "I know God showed you something. Would you come to the platform to share it with the whole church?" I told him that I would.

I shared all that I had seen with the congregation. Then, I pointed at the little gray-haired lady. "This is for you, but we can all learn from it, too." As soon as I told her, she jumped to her feet and praised God! It was a great change for her; a life changing way of life for her. After church, she thanked me and said she felt wonderful. She finally felt a peace that her children would be saved. She finally believed it *and* received it.

UNCLE HUCK

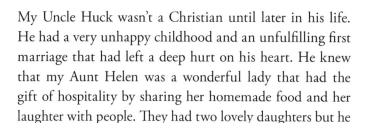

My Uncle Huck wasn't a Christian until later in his life. He had a very unhappy childhood and an unfulfilling first marriage that had left a deep hurt on his heart. He knew that my Aunt Helen was a wonderful lady that had the gift of hospitality by sharing her homemade food and her laughter with people. They had two lovely daughters but he was disappointed that they didn't have a son. His daughters grew up feeling he had rejected them.

Aunt Helen and their daughters loved the Lord and were good people, but my uncle didn't go anywhere with them. Even though he loved his wife, he didn't buy her any gifts. It seemed that he was determined to stay "stuck" in disappointment and he let that feeling overtake his life. He had been married before and it had been full of hurt and pain and misplaced trust. Unfortunately, because of all that hurt he experienced, Aunt Helen paid the price for his disastrous first marriage. After many years of living like this, he began not feeling well and he entered the hospital. Tests revealed that he had cancer.

I went to the hospital with my Aunt Helen and Cousin Sandra to offer a prayer for him. After we talked for awhile, he accepted Jesus Christ as his Savior, but he told me that he had made peace with God and didn't want to stay on this earth. He desired to go to Heaven. He didn't want to receive a miracle to live here. He had asked God if he could go, and God told him that he could. He wanted me to tell his family after he went home to be with the Lord.

When I prayed for him, I prayed for God's perfect will to be done, but I really wanted him to receive his healing and then able to show my Aunt Helen and both his daughters the love that they had missed. The next day he was dead. I was able to tell them what he'd shared with me. We were all disappointed he wasn't here anymore, but we rejoiced that he accepted Christ and was in Heaven now.

About a year had passed when I saw a vision of Uncle Huck. He was smiling while standing there in a gorgeous white robe. "Tell your Aunt Helen it will be better for us when she comes to heaven."

I told her what I saw and heard. She said, "Yeah, right." She didn't believe what he'd told me because she couldn't figure out how that would be possible.

Years later, my Aunt Helen died suddenly due to heart failure. I saw her at Heaven's Gate looking so young and full of energy. Uncle Huck greeted her at the iridescent Gate of Pearl. "Helen, I'm glad you're here", he said. "Things won't be the same here like they were on earth. I'm sorry." He put his arm around her lovingly as they walked on the gold street, showing me their beautiful white robes. I was impressed with how young and healthy they both looked. They radiated with such energy. A bright white light shone all around them. Their robes had long sleeves and came down to their feet. Uncle Huck had brown sandals on his feet. Aunt Helen looked like she had on flat shoes that looked like white satin to me. I really don't know the material and wasn't told what it was.

A fragrance filled the air that smelled like a light sweet smell, like a mixture of delightful flowers. Roses and lavender stood out in my mind the most. Every time I saw a vision of Heaven, I wanted to stay there with its wonderful fragrances everywhere. There were different aromas in different areas with so much beauty to see and saints to talk to. Everyone was willing to talk and has so much love. The love is so strong that you can tangibly feel it.

Angels have a tremendous part in doing things. There are more angels than you'd ever imagine; assigned to do different things. God hasn't left anything out. Praises to God and to Jesus Christ are heard everywhere. You can hear singing also. I even heard singing in the River of Life. I could go on and on, but the love and peace were the most extraordinary things that I cherished. God is so perfect; He doesn't need to change. He is so knowledgeable, and no one compares to Him. I can honestly say that Heaven is a real place, and you don't want to miss it!

Schooling

A few years passed, and I saw a vision of a couple in Heaven. They were talking while they stood on a street of gold. Their backs were facing me and I heard them softly laughing. I overheard him ask her, "May I carry that for you?"

She giggled like a young girl and answered, "Sure." I was curious what she was holding. They were acting like two teenagers in love. I thought their voices sounded familiar, so I asked the angel if I could go in front of them to see who they were. And I still wanted to know what she held in her hand that he was willing to carry. I was permitted to go around to the front of them. Well, this is a surprise! It was my Uncle Huck and Aunt Helen.

I don't know if they saw me because they didn't say anything to me, nor did I say anything to them. Surprise wasn't exactly the word I should have used. It would be more accurate to say that I was absolutely astonished! I had never seen them act so much in love with one another while they were on earth. Aunt Helen handed him a white Bible that had his name on it, written in gold letters. Then, they held hands as they were walking on the gold street. I noticed how young they looked. They had on white robes. Aunt Helen had short, curly, brown hair. Uncle Huck had dark brown hair and all the gray that had been in his hair was completely gone.

They radiated with a joy I hadn't seen them have the entire time I knew them both. I felt so happy seeing them together. I praised God and knew I had witnessed a miracle from God. A couple restored with a tremendous love for one another. I asked the angel, "Where are they going?"

"They're going to school to learn about the Bible", he said. I was surprised again. I thought that once we got to Heaven it was more or less a playground because I had never thought about it, I guess.

The Word of God is forever. It's for all eternity. There is so much we don't know here on earth. Learning the Word of God is not a chore, but a gift. What we learn there we will always know. No one is plagued by forgetfulness. Praise God! The Fruits of the Spirit are in operation there, so of course the gifts of the Spirit, such as wisdom and knowledge would be evident. I had never thought of it that way before.

Galatians 5:22 (KJV)

But the fruit of the Spirit is love, joy, peace, longsuffering, gentleness, goodness, faith.

I asked God about the longsuffering. "For now, waiting on loved ones to get here; I'm longing for the day I know they will be here. Suffering on earth is different than Heaven. Suffering on earth is what you go through; it's the trials that you live through and endure. Suffering in Heaven means you know you already came through things and appreciate God for His help. Your troubles and being sick are behind you", he said to me.

There were other subjects we discussed, and I will share another part of this conversation near the end of the book. You will understand His heart better, I think, if I save it until the end. Once God and I finished our conversation, the angel brought me back home.

The angel had told me that there was a school, but I had never seen one. It was now close to Father's Day. I asked God what my dad was doing up in Heaven and would He show me.

On Father's Day, early in the morning, at 3:00 a.m., He showed me a vision. I was standing in Heaven, outside a door. The angel opened the door, and I saw a classroom with desks. My dad was sitting at the back of the room. I know he saw me, but he didn't speak so we wouldn't interrupt the class. Every seat was filled with saints. An angel who looked about eight feet tall was standing at a chalkboard with a pointer. He had written the Word of God on it and was explaining what it meant. The angel didn't speak to me, but he smiled at me knowing God had allowed me to see the class and my dad. He knew I was to write what I saw about the school.

Whatever you don't know about the Bible here on earth you will learn there, starting with the first page. You will learn everything about that page that God wants you to know. Once you learn it, you won't forget it. Page by page, you will be taught. I asked the angel who was with me about the saints that have been in Heaven for a long time.

"Will they ever know all of the Bible?"

"There is so much to learn, but through all eternity we will never know all the knowledge that God knows," he told me.

God taught the angels what He wanted them to teach the saints about His Word. They teach on each page until you understand what God desires you to know.

AUNT HELEN

One day, I asked God what my Aunt Helen was doing. She had been gone awhile now and I missed her so much. I was allowed to see her in Heaven.

I asked, "Are you as happy as you look?"

She smiled at me. "I'm very happy here," she replied.

Aunt Helen was wearing a royal blue robe with shoes to match. She showed me a beautiful big blue diamond that she was wearing on her finger.

"Why are you wearing blue? I thought all robes were white."

"This is my choir robe and my choir ring."

Aunt Helen loved to sing while she was on earth, so I am not surprised that she's singing in the choir in Heaven.

Did not the father of the lost son in the Bible put a ring on his son's finger? And God will give us a ring also as our Heavenly Father. It will be part of our reward. All the jewels will be different.

UNCLE HUCK

"God, you showed me what my Aunt Helen was doing. Will you show me what my Uncle Huck is doing??

He showed me a vision of Heaven. I saw a huge room with every kind of paint; watercolors and oils of every color as well as pencils, rulers, brushes and every other kind of supply you would need to draw and paint. Canvas boards and frames of all sizes for painting and drawing were there. Everything was neatly in its place.

I was looking around when I saw my Uncle Huck standing in front of a huge table with some kind of paper on it. He was painting a mural on it. I was standing to the side with my back towards the front of the building, so I couldn't see what he was drawing or painting. The angel was standing beside me.

"Am I allowed to see what he's drawing?"

"No one will see it but your Uncle and God. God asked him to paint it for Him. He gave him his talent to draw and you can use your talents in Heaven. This painting will be put in God's house. The angels will transport it there."

Let me tell you that I never knew my Uncle Huck could draw. When the vision was over, I called one of Uncle Huck's daughters to tell her what I had seen. She told me an amazing, true story.

When her dad was very young, he could look at anything and draw it. When he was in high school, the teacher wanted him to go to art school in New York City. His dad was a very abusive man and forbid him to go, so he didn't. He gave up his dream of doing anything with his art.

He drew cartoons for his two little girls when they were little, but my cousin didn't know that he ever did anything else with his talent except drawing those cartoons for them. Hearing about his life, I thought about him having an abusive dad that didn't give him any encouragement or confidence to use his talent, but here in Heaven I saw him so radiated with joy and at peace as he was making a huge mural for God, his Heavenly Father.

Psalm 37:4-5

4 Delight thyself also in the Lord; and He shall give thee the desires of thine heart. 5 Commit thy way unto the Lord, trust also in Him, and He shall bring it to pass.

Even in Heaven, God gives us our hearts' desires. Each saint is so special to God. It made me want to praise Him more.

My Cousin Sandra

Sandra was a great prayer warrior because she had such compassion and love for people. We were first cousins, but felt like sisters. Later in her life, she developed a growth on her shoulder. The doctor diagnosed her with Stage 4 cancer. She couldn't raise her arm. Cancer spread quickly throughout her body.

At 8:30 one Friday morning, I had gotten dressed and was standing in front of the mirror getting ready to brush my hair. I felt Sandra's presence, so I turned around expecting to see her. She wasn't there, but I smelled a sweet spice fragrance. The scent filled the room, but I didn't know what it meant, so I asked God. He told me Sandra's body was shutting down at the nursing home and that she'd been talking to Him. After I prayed, I opened my eyes and saw a vision.

I saw Sandra with her natural color of medium brown short hair. Her hair looked so wavy and luscious. She was her perfect weight and radiated with joy. She was beautiful as I saw her in her flowing white robe. What a sight to see my cousin fly towards her mom (Aunt Helen) to embrace her, as her mother stood waiting for her daughter at the entrance of the Gate of Pearl in Heaven. Her dad (Uncle Huck) was standing to the right of her. Sandra's mom and Uncle Clarence were standing to her left. (Sandra and her sister, Marilyn, had led their uncle to the Lord before he died.) They were talking but I don't know what they said. The vision left. I was looking in the mirror once again.

"Lord, should I call her sister to tell what I've just seen?"

"Wait," was the answer.

I went on to minister at a nursing home since they were expecting me. At 11:20 that morning, my cell phone rang. It was my cousin, Marilyn, telling me the nurse where Sandra was at had called her. She told her Sandra had just died. I understood why God had allowed me to see the vision. I could share it with her so that she wouldn't feel guilty for not seeing Sandra earlier that morning. Sandra wouldn't have known that she was there.

It took time for the nursing home to have the doctor check Sandra, call the coroner, and then call Marilyn. That is the grace of God at work.

Several days later, I saw a vision of Sandra. She was standing with her back to me and her dad was standing to her left. He had his hand on her shoulder.

He was talking to her and said, "You know I love you."

"I always felt you resented me because I wasn't a boy and that made me feel rejected", she told him.

"That was true. We're in Heaven now, so I won't lie about it, but I've been forgiven. I do love you." He put his arm around her shoulder.

Her mother came up to her right side and put her arm around Sandra and said, "You'll love it here. We have so many things to show you."

"I already do," Sandra spoke softly.

Watching that scene, I was overcome with the grace and the mercy of God for my loved ones.

SEEING A FRIEND

I lived in North Carolina and was invited to go to a wedding in Ohio. I packed my suitcase for a week, thinking that I would be home when the week was over. The night before I left, I heard the Lord speak to me that I should pack enough clothes for two weeks, although I didn't know why, since he didn't tell me. My phone rang and it was my cousin, Marilyn, asking me if I'd like to visit her and her family for a week. If so, they would pick me up after the reception was over. Not being in Ohio for years, they wanted to show me all the changes around the places I'd been used to seeing.

We attended the beautiful wedding and then I left with my cousin and her family. It was amazing to see the old neighborhood and the changes that had been made. Marilyn asked me if I'd like to visit my sister in Kentucky.

I sure did! We left the next morning. We had a great visit, talking and catching up with each other. I was asked to visit a friend of mine that I hadn't seen in many years. She had been diagnosed with cancer and was not doing well at all.

When I arrived, the first thing she did was smile and say, "I prayed you'd come to see me because I need to talk to you."

I was very surprised because when I left Ohio to come visit my sister, I had no idea that I would be seeing her.

"I heard you had cancer, and I prayed for you. The Lord told me you wouldn't accept a miracle because you gave up. You've chosen to die."

"That's right, but God won't take me. I want you to tell me why."

I had to pray. She told me she had doubts she'd go to Heaven. She professed Christianity so I was concerned about her remarks. When I asked her why she thought I had her answer, she said that when she prayed God showed her my face, so she prayed God would bring me to see her. She was in a hospital bed in her living room and couldn't get to me.

I was amazed, but silently prayed for her.

"Who are you angry at?" When I went down the list, it wasn't her family, friends, neighbors or enemies on her part. That left God.

"Are you made at God?" I asked.

"Yes, I am."

"Do you mind telling me why?"

"Nothing worked out right in my life. Now, I have cancer and I'm dying. And He won't let me go to Heaven."

Let me tell you, I prayed. This lady needed an answer.

"God told me you didn't ask Him ahead about your life or what you should do in your circumstances. You made your own messes", I finally said.

"That's true," was her quiet reply.

"You're being angry at God caused bitterness; bitterness caused unforgiveness. With unforgiveness, if you died, you'd go to Hell. God said in His Word, 'if we don't forgive others, He won't forgive us.' Without forgiveness, He can't accept you into Heaven. He means what He said, and He said what He means."

Without forgiveness, we must remember, there is no peace.

I didn't have time for her to tell me every detail of her life, nor was it any of my business. She thought about what I'd told her. It took a while for her to think about what she wanted to do.

"I forgive God. Will He forgive me?" she asked.

"Yes," I replied. "He will. He's been waiting on you, or He wouldn't have sent me to tell you."

"What's next?" she asked

I prayed for her and we both felt a tremendous peace come upon us. We were saturated in the wonderful peace of God.

Then God told me to tell her not to be afraid when she passed over to Heaven. He'd send three angels for her. She cried. She was so happy! Then she praised God because she thought she would go alone.

Her daughter called me twelve days later to tell me that she had died. Close to her dying, her family could tell she was looking at something but they didn't know what. They asked her if she was seeing Jesus Christ.

She replied, "Yes, yes, yes," and she was gone.

I told her daughter what had happened when I had been there talking and ministering to her. If she'd just seen Jesus

Christ, she would only have said one yes. Saying yes three times was for each of the three angels. She knew I'd tell them when the time was right.

The Bible story of Stephen being stoned told us that he saw Jesus Christ. Why am I writing this in the book? It's wonderful to have a part in God's plan for someone to come to Him or to make peace with Him. Maybe someone will know how serious God feels about unforgiveness. Repent and go on. What I thought was going to be a wedding in Ohio became a reuniting of a soul back to God in Kentucky.

I thanked my cousin and her family for taking me there. Do you think they will be surprised when they receive a reward in Heaven for the part that they played in all this? I do!

God answered my friend's prayer, and it was worth the trip. I thought about it later, Jesus Christ's first miracle was at a wedding. My friend received miracles and salvation. Entering Heaven she was made whole. And now she is with Christ for all of eternity. It was definitely worth the trip.

A few days later, I saw a vision of my friend, my sister in the Lord, in Heaven. She looked beautiful in her white robe, standing with a saint I didn't know, holding hands. The one I didn't know looked like she was about seventeen. They were just smiling at each other, not speaking. I noticed that the younger one looked perfect. Within a few seconds I knew she had Down Syndrome and then she would look perfect again. The older one, my friend, thanked me for praying and talking to her before she died.

I called my friend's daughter to share what I had seen. I didn't understand why I thought the young saint with my friend had Down Syndrome. There isn't any sickness or disabilities of any kind in Heaven. "I can explain", she said. "My mother had a sister that died when she was seventeen of Down Syndrome. We didn't know if she could comprehend salvation and wondered if she went to Heaven. You confirmed it. I can tell the family now."

I'm reminded of how Jesus Christ was surrounded by the crowds in the Bible, but I'm amazed how I see Jesus Christ minister to the one that needs Him the most. Please don't take God's Word lightly. He's a Holy God and we must obey Him and not man.

I love to read about Moses and David in the Bible. They were both men who had great adventures. They experienced triumphs with God and things didn't go nearly so well when God wasn't in their exploits. We can all learn from that. And Moses saw great miracles while helping the children of Israel make their way to the Promised Land. Although we may live in a natural world, we serve a supernatural God and I have seen Him do supernatural things myself. Reading about Moses helps me to increase my faith about some of the things that I can believe God for. And the Psalms are so beautiful and one of my favorite books of the Bible; full of both despair and praise. Even in some of the worse times of his life, David learned to praise God. Being a praiser like David, I am drawn to that book. I've used the Book of Psalms many times over the years as I have taught and ministered to people.

Psalm 72:18 (KJV)

Blessed be the Lord God, the God of Israel
who only doeth wondrous things.

SEEING ANOTHER PART OF HEAVEN

I was always amazed at seeing Heaven. This time the angel took me to the Gate of Pearl, which I had seen before, but King David was standing there holding a golden harp.

"I didn't know you had a little harp," I said to David. The angel told me he was going to be my tour guide.

David was wearing a white robe all trimmed with gold and wearing a big gold belt buckle that had an emblem on it. He had a serious personality. David was standing to my right. To my left was Moses. These are my favorites when I read from the Bible. I liked them being leaders to new adventures. David wrote the majority of the Psalms, and Psalms is one of my favorite books, so this was going to be a real treat for me.

I said to Moses, "I didn't know you were so short."

"Most people say that," Moses replied grinning. Moses had a great sense of humor. His robe was different than David's. Stripes were going down it in colors of blue, green and gold. It looked like real gold threads running throughout the entire garment, from the top to the bottom of each stripe.

I asked the angel, "Why are their robes so different?"

"David is a King, and Moses is a Prophet."

It was time for the angel, David, and I to walk through the gate onto the street of gold, which looked like transparent glass. Moses stayed behind as we went to the right, to the River of Life, where I saw light blue water that was so clear that I could see down deeply into it. I got in and then back out to see if my robe was wet. I don't know when a robe was put on me, but I saw it at the River of Life. The angel knew I was joking and told me to get back into the water and take deep breaths because I would need the strength. I obeyed. I re-entered the river and got myself under the water. I took a few deep breaths. I didn't take water into my lungs, like I would have on earth. Instead, my lungs were filled with air that was filled with a vibrant energy. I immediately was refreshed! When I came back up out of the water, I saw a red bird over my head and heard him chirping. Then he flew away.

Other people were further ahead of me. I had my eyes open and could see. I could hear singing but I didn't know what they were singing. I wanted to know how deep the River of Life was, but I really couldn't tell. The angel said that we had been summoned, so I had to get out. The word summoned is used a lot in Heaven, as I would come to realize.

I didn't have wings, but the angel put his arm around me and we flew to the left and stopped. A big white house with a few steps and a big porch was to my left. The door opened and I saw my Grandmother. She was smiling at us. She had died before I was born but I had seen her picture so I knew that she was my mom's mother. They looked so much alike.

We entered into her foyer. The angel, David, my grandmother, and I were all standing on what looked like one gigantic piece of white marble with a round circle of red roses with tiny emerald green leaves. The artwork was so intricate that the roses and leaves looked real.

"How did you do this?" I asked.

She replied, "The children came here and did this for me."

I didn't understand at all.

We walked into the living room. All of her furniture, rugs and walls were white with gold trim. It was stunningly beautiful. Now, I knew where my love for white came from. It would be great if I could have seen her whole house, sat down and talked, have so many of my questions answered, maybe even get some hugs and kisses, but it didn't happen. I asked her "Can I see your house?" (I'd like to make a comment here. I'm surprised what I could have asked instead of what I actually did say. I love to see interior design, so I believe that's why I said that, instead of starting on my other questions.) That didn't happen either. I didn't get a tour of the house like I was hoping to. Instead, we were back at the front door.

I looked at my grandmother and asked, "Do you ever see my Aunt Helen (her daughter)?

"Yes, when she isn't doing other things."

"Do you ever see my Uncle Huck?" She smiled, but David told me we were summoned to go now.

"I've always loved and missed you", I said

She smiled and nodded to me.

David looked at me and said, "God has a surprise for you."

We flew to another white building. The speed was so fast that I didn't know how far we had gone. We were just there. Inside, front and center, was a podium with a big white Bible on it. HOLY BIBLE was written with gold letters. The edges of the pages were some kind of paper, which I believed to be expensive parchment. All the lettering was done in real gold. My Uncle Huck was there and he flew up to the top of the shelves to show me that he had his sense of humor. I laughed out loud.

"Why are all the books here?" I asked.

Rows and rows of bookshelves were there. From the ceiling to the floor and all around the room, the shelves were filled with books.

"This looks like a library," I said.

"It is a library. All the talents you have on earth that God gave you; you can use them here. Saints can write poems, songs, plays, skits and whatever else they write about," replied Uncle Huck.

We had to leave to go to another building. It looked like a factory to me. I saw screwdrivers, hammers, saws, etc. Everything was clean and quiet so there was no dust or noise. An angel carried a small white foyer-table, trimmed in gold, out the door. I asked where he was taking it and was told it was going to my grandmother's house because she asked for it. That's awesome! Our heart's desire is fulfilled even in Heaven!

David said we had to go. We flew to an outside amphitheater. There was a sense of excitement everywhere. I wondered what was going on. All ages of children were there. There were children on the platform. Angels flew in and it got quiet. I don't know what was said, but from the oldest to the youngest, the children lined up two by two. The angels were on the outside of all the children with one angel in front and one angel at the rear. David told me I had to go back to the River of Life because I'd need to receive strength again. We were going to the Throne of God.

I want to stop here and explain something very important to you. The angel told me I was allowed to go to the Throne of God because I fellowshipped with God all the time and I was a praiser. I frequently praise God out loud. If you are shy and can't praise out loud, you will have to go to school to learn how to praise out loud before you can go into the Throne Room. It is an awesome place to be, but very loud because all the saints in there are praising God out loud at the same time.

I got in the River of Life again and took several big breaths. Then we flew towards the right and it seemed we were slightly going up. I could hear what seemed to me to be multitudes of praises getting louder and louder as we were entering a room.

Suddenly, I could see rows of saints with spaces in front of them. I wondered why. As we watched everyone in their own way, praising God in unison, I would hear "Alleluia!"

It was always Alleluia and never pronounced with an H. Someone would praise God and fall on their face before Him, then stand up and praise Him again. That's why there were the spaces between the rows.

As I moved closer to the front, I wasn't able to see God for all the brightness of the light. White light was all around Him. I saw emerald green light mixed with white above Him. There were colors of pink, yellow, blue and green; those were off to the side. I did see the bottom of a white robe from the knees down to His feet. His feet were a brown color, just like the Jewish people I have seen.

I did see part of a beautiful white chair. The arms of the chair were carved like the head of a lion. The eyes looked like a real red ruby and it was etched with real gold. A large space was in the front of God. I was wondering why when I looked and saw the angels flying with the children from the amphitheater. They were still two by two in a line. The oldest children went to the back row, while the smallest ones were in the front row. The youngest were toddlers who could talk. Their speech was perfect. With smiles on their faces, they praised God in their own way. What an awesome sight to see and hear all of these children, all these various ages, and to hear them praise God with such joy. You cannot be there and not want to praise God yourself.

Above the Throne were tiny spirits. God's voice sounded like thunder when He spoke. It was a deep, smooth voice, but He spoke with such authority. The best way I know how to describe it is that His voice was like water rippling.

"Will a child go to a family? You will be a special child. You will have a handicap. Who will go and be this special child? This child will bring the parents to Jesus Christ and to me."

A tiny spirit would say, "I will go! Please send me."

God would say, "Go now." And whoosh--God's arm would extend, and away the tiny spirit would go with an angel. I knew they were headed to earth. Three times I heard this about different situations and the tiny spirits would go with the angels. I don't know how or what happened after they left because I wasn't told. The angel with me told me I had to go after I said praises to God because He wanted to show me more of Heaven.

We flew out and went before an enormous white house. It had pillars in the front with a big door.

I asked the angel, "Who lives there? They must have fulfilled a big ministry for God."

I asked if I could go inside and see it.

The angel said, "No one ever goes inside this house but God, because it's God's house."

I was amazed! I cannot comprehend how God can sit on His Throne in Heaven, knows everything that goes on there, on earth, in Hell and everywhere else, and still have time to go to His house. When I asked the angel he said, "Because He is God."

It was time for us to go. I wasn't told where we were going, but the angel and David were always with me. On our way, we saw a mother, father, and a child with a picnic basket. I asked the angel where they were going and was told they were going on a picnic. I asked if we could go with them. I felt disappointed when I was told we couldn't go.

We stopped and were waiting with other saints when it looked like a white airplane, without any wings, came to where we were standing. Everyone standing there got inside. You talk about a fast ride! It was the fastest ride I had ever been on in my life. It felt like we went straight, then curved to the left and stopped. When we got out, I saw the prettiest white snow that I have ever seen. I asked the angel where we were.

"In the mountains," he said.

I had always thought that the atmosphere in the mountains would be cold because there is snow on the mountains, but it wasn't cold at all. There were many saints laughing and throwing snowballs at each other. They seemed to be having quite a bit of fun. What amazed me was the snow. When it fell back to the ground, it was perfect; if you stepped on it, you couldn't see any foot prints. It wasn't mush, and there was no ice anywhere. I was told that the Eskimos loved to live in the mountains, but I didn't see their houses. I touched the snow. It wasn't cold as I held it.

We waited for the white airplane to come back to where we were to get us. Inside, we flew at a rapid speed straight ahead and curved to the right and then we were back where we started. I didn't think to ask what it was called. Back home, of course, I thought of many questions I wish I would have asked, but when new sights and sounds seem to be coming at you so fast, it's hard to comprehend it all, let alone ask questions about everything.

David told me that we were going to see the Wedding Setting. We flew with the angel to a different place. I can't tell you where it was. We arrived to see angels flying around busily preparing a room full of tables. Tables were set with white tablecloths embroidered with gold threads. There were red glasses and plates that had a hint of gold to them and another blue glass with a gold cast to them. Big blue bowls were sitting in the middle of the tables and gold silverware was at each place setting. There were also some gold bowls with a hint of green on the tables. Such a colorful table setting! With all the colors and the precision of all the place settings, I know it was the prettiest table setting that I had ever seen.

David told me that when a sinner gets saved, an angel goes to put another setting on the table. The Marriage Supper setting has already been prepared, so that when the saints are there it will be ready for all of us.

There is no night in Heaven and those who live there do not sleep. Each day has a quiet time to rest. This, as in every other aspect of Heaven, has an order to it. I didn't want to leave. I wanted to stay there forever, but the angel told me it was my time to leave. We flew back to the gate, which was the entrance we came in.

Thanking David and feeling sad I had to leave, the angel and I rapidly flew back to earth. I can't wait until I can go back to stay.

BETTY

Betty was my sister-in-law whom I loved dearly and we prayed together many times throughout the years. She lived in Florida and came to see me in North Carolina one summer.

The Lord told me that she wouldn't be here for Christmas. He was taking her to Heaven. Later, it was close to Christmas and I was listening to Christmas music playing on the radio. All of a sudden, the ceiling became a bright white light, so I looked up. Betty was standing there straight and beautiful in a white robe. She smiled at me and said, "I love you." Then she was gone. I looked at the clock, and it was 11:10 a.m.

I called my sister Thelma, to tell her about what I had seen. Then I called another sister, Lorine, to tell her what I had seen, as well. Once phone calls were made by my sisters, it was found out that her burial was at 11:00 a.m. that day. Right before Christmas, as God had told me, Betty went home to her eternal reward.

GLORIA

Tired, I had gone to bed early, only to wake up at 3:00 in the morning to see my ceiling a bright white. I could hardly see in the dark room. I squinted my eyes to see my niece, Gloria. She had died a few years ago.

"I asked the Lord to let me see you. Thanks for letting me see you", I said to her.

"I have a message for you. Tell my sister that I'm here and I'm happy. She wants to come here, but it isn't time for her yet. Tell her to be happy. I saw Larry (Gloria's husband). I know he's remarried. It's alright."

"Where do you live?" I quickly asked her.

"With my mother, Stella (my sister)." I asked her who all she saw in our family that I knew. She named a long list of people.

She said, "God let me see you today for one of your Christmas gifts." She told me about some situations I needed to know about in my life. When it was over, I called some of the family to tell them I had seen her. Praise God!

THE CHEROKEE WOMAN

Another time, the Lord told me he wanted to show me something in Heaven. Sometimes I know the purpose for being allowed to go, and sometimes God surprises me with everything I see. It's very hard to describe all the beauty that is everywhere. The colors that we have here simply pale in comparison to the vibrant color that is there. Since there is no dust or pollution there, the air that we breathe here, even in the most remote locations, does not compare to the air there. There is no sin, no pollution, no cuss words or pornography. Everything is so clean and orderly and there is so much to do and to see. Everyone is healthy and their bodies are whole. They are happy, productive, learning, using their gifts and most importantly, they are loving God and praising Him and His dear son for all that He's done.

You can think a thought to the one that you are with and the saint understands. They communicate spirit to spirit, without lips having to move to communicate the thought. There is a knowing in the spirit realm, as I have mentioned before, but I don't know how to explain more fully.

I entered Heaven and had gone through the pearl gate once again. I passed the gold streets, through the city to the left and saw the most gorgeous clear blue lake that was enormous. It had the prettiest light blue water that I had ever seen. As I stood there looking at it, I felt very peaceful. The beauty of it all amazed me.

As I looked far across the lake, I saw a white canoe with what appeared to have a woman sitting in it. I kept my eyes watching her as the canoe moved slowly across the water towards me. No sound was heard, nor did I see any motors or oars being rowed with it. Indian designs were on the outside at the back of the canoe. The closer the canoe came to me I could see this woman more clearly. She was absolutely beautiful. She looked young with black straight hair that came down to her waist.

We didn't speak to each other, but I looked at her deep brown eyes as she looked into my eyes. I felt that she knew me and loved me. I dearly loved her, too, but wondered what the connection was between us.

Looking behind me, I saw elegant Indian-style stucco houses that were all made close together on the outside. Each one had an arched doorway and there were Indian designs of red, green, blue and yellow, although I didn't know what any of the symbols and designs meant, and I wasn't told. She had red, green, blue and yellow designs on the front of her gown, too.

I asked the angel with me, "Where are we?"

"We're at the lake. The Indians love to live near the water."

In awe of everything that I saw, I finally realized I was back at my house still wondering who that saint was, and what connection she had with me.

"God, who was that lady?" I asked Him.

"She's your great-grandmother. She wanted to meet you and you wanted to meet her."

All of my grandparents had died before I was born, and I had asked God if I could see them in Heaven many times over many years.

I felt led to call one of my older sisters to tell her. When I explained what I saw, she said that she could tell me who the Indian lady was. The Indian lady was our dad's grandmother, so she would, indeed, by our great-grandmother, just as God had said. She was a full Cherokee Indian from North Carolina that was taken to Tennessee to live before she died. My dad had never shared our Indian heritage with me so I had no idea. No wonder I couldn't make a connection as to who this woman was and why we had such a strong connection.

How I longed to stay in Heaven to talk to her, to give her a hug and to hear all that she could tell me, but I wasn't permitted to stay long enough for any of that. The pull to stay there, in that atmosphere of love and peace is so strong that I never want to leave there. You won't feel the love down here like you'll feel when you get to Heaven.

BOB

Bob was in the hospital for a minor operation. However, he took a turn for the worse and I received a call to pray for him. As I was praying, I saw a vision.

Bob was lying in his hospital bed in a coma. His eyes were shut. Jesus Christ walked into his hospital room. The conversation went like this:

"Bob, do you know who I am?"

"Are you Jesus Christ?"

"Yes, I am. Are you ready to go now?"

"Where are you talking about me going? If you want me well and going back to my house, I'm afraid that I can't live a holy life, but I don't want to go to Hell."

"I'm talking about going with me to Heaven now."

"What about my wife and my brother?" Bob asked

"I'll take care of them."

"I'm ready. I'm tired of the pain."

Jesus took Bob by the hand, and he got out of the bed and had a white robe on—made whole by Jesus Christ! They flew out of the room together. Bob was smiling and talking as they left.

In the hallway of the hospital, I saw his wife talking with her sister about Christ. I knew she would be all right. And his brother would be, too. He won't be left behind because God answers prayers. I know Bob went with Jesus Christ to Heaven.

I called to tell one of my cousins what I had seen. She said at the time I saw the vision, she was at the hospital and knew Bob was in a coma. She was concerned about his salvation and had prayed for him. And his wife's sister was in the hallway talking to her about her salvation. She accepted Christ, as well.

What a Savior!

A YOUNG GIRL

At a church I attended for awhile, a seventeen year old girl had been involved in a car accident and had died not that long ago. I was in one of the regular church services praising God when I saw Jesus Christ, His mother, Mary, and the young girl in-between them, standing on the platform. Mary had a pink chiffon scarf on that was very long and it started to blow as if the wind was picking up. She told me to "take the wind of the Holy Spirit to the people." I responded that I would tell the ones who were in authority at the church. Then, Mary told me to tell the girl's mother that she would help to look after her daughter and for her not to worry. Her daughter was awaiting her arrival in Heaven. She was well and safe.

Her mother wasn't at church that particular day, but when I saw her later I did tell her what I had seen. She cried as she told me that hearing that had made her so happy. She had worried, but felt at peace now. She hugged me and thanked me. I always marvel when God uses me to show the goodness of God to one of His children.

Once, I shared this story at a prayer group. A woman that was there didn't like it. She asked me, "Who are you that you would see the mother of my Lord? You aren't even Catholic!"

"Only a child of God, I replied. "I saw what He wanted me to see."

I have no doubt that the reason I am to write this book is to share with everyone what I have been privileged enough to see. Hopefully, it will bring comfort and joy to those who have lost loved ones in death to know that they aren't in pain anymore; but are healthy, whole and happy once again. It is not to bring any sort of glory to me, but to bring glory to my Heavenly Father by showing His great and enduring love for us.

CHRISTMAS MUSIC AND MOM

It was July 17, 2008, the day after mom died. I was lying on my bed when I heard beautiful music. A woman's voice was singing, "Silent Night, Holy Night. All is calm, all is bright." I was wondering why the family was playing Christmas music in July. I got up, left my bedroom, went to the living room and went into my daughter's living room. To my surprise, there was no radio, internet or compact discs playing anywhere in here. I had family visiting here from out of state. I thought that perhaps they must have stayed up all night long to be up this early in the morning. I walked around the house and realized that they were all asleep. Amazing!

The music was gone now. I went back to my bedroom quietly, thinking, "Silent Night...but Lord, this is early morning." I thought how silent the house was. I had to admit I felt the presence of the Lord, so the Holy Night began to make some sense to me. It didn't have to be Christmas to feel the presence of the Lord.

All is calm. I was so close to and loved my mom so much that everyone thought that I would crash when mom died. To be honest, I wondered if I would, too. I had prayed ahead of time. And I knew a lot of family and friends were praying for me. It was amazing to see how everyone, including myself, had gone through it all as calm as we did. Making all the arrangements went smoothly. Hospice was wonderful to us and had a beautiful service for her. It was calm.

All is bright. No devil, sickness, or person could ever hurt my mom again. She's with Christ, at peace and with her body made whole. Once she was blind, but now her eyes can see perfectly. Her false teeth didn't fit because of a stroke, but now her teeth have been restored. She walked with a limp in one leg, now she walks perfectly straight without the slightest limp at all. She has family in Heaven and family here on earth. Mom is with her Savior and friend, the Lord Jesus Christ, whom she loved most of all. I miss her more than words can say. My hope is being with her for all eternity someday.

While still lying on my bed, I said, "Lord, I so much want to see my mom. What is she doing? Who is she with?"

Immediately I was shown into Heaven. She had her back to me. She was slender and beautiful, with medium brown hair that was short and curly. I immediately knew it was her. I didn't know why I wasn't allowed to see her face. Standing in a circle, was my first husband, Randy, my dad, Aunt Helen, Uncle Clarence, and a man that I didn't recognize.

I could hear my Uncle Huck's voice, but I didn't understand the words he spoke. Everyone was laughing. Randy was laughing so hard that he would bend down at the waist and then straighten back up, all the while laughing. All the years I had known that man, I had never seen him laugh like that. Wondering what was so funny, I asked God, but He didn't tell me. Uncle Huck was standing next to my mom with his back to me as well. The Lord spoke to me and told me that the man that I didn't know was my mom's brother.

Years ago, my mom told me a true story from many years back. When her mother, Florence, my grandmother, was a young married woman, she had a three-week old baby boy. A flood came through Dayton, Ohio, where they were living at the time. Boats were there to get them to safety. The men were in one boat and the women were helped to get in another boat. Florence's husband had their baby boy and bent down to hand him to Florence, when water gushed by, rocking the boat and causing him to drop the baby. The choppy and rapidly moving water quickly took the baby underwater and he was never seen again. It is assumed, of course, that he had drowned.

I was told by the Lord that he had indeed drowned and was taken to Heaven. He was the guy that I saw. He had grown up to be a handsome man. Uncle Clarence looked a lot like his older brother. I don't know why, but I wasn't told his name or explained why I wasn't told. I'm looking forward to the day that I can see and be with them. I know I will.

According to the Bible, there is no sadness in Heaven. We can't comprehend all the happiness that is there. I don't know what the future holds for me, but with God's help, it will be calm and bright.

FLOYD IN HEAVEN

This isn't a vision that I personally had, so I thought twice about including it. But, it happened to someone very close to me and I did decide to include it here because I know this man and his integrity and thought it was worth sharing.

My new husband, Floyd, wasn't feeling well, so he took his blood pressure. His pulse was 150 so he went to see the doctor. The doctor sent him immediately to the hospital where they gave him medicine that raced his heart too much. So they gave him different medicine, which slowed it down.

He began to see a vision. The wall across from him looked like thousands of people committing sins. He wondered why he had seen it, unless he was supposed to pray for them, although he didn't know them. He asked me if I saw it, which I didn't. But as I watched him, he took his last breath and died. Nurses and doctors surrounded him and worked on him. No paddles were used to bring him back to life. After seventeen minutes he came back and was telling us what he saw.

"I don't know where I was, but I thought I was in heaven. It was so white all around me that I could hardly see. I never saw a white as bright as that before. I heard someone talking, but I didn't understand what they were saying. I said, 'What am I doing here?' I didn't see anyone, but I heard a voice that said, 'What do you want?' I said, 'You didn't let me finish my ministry.' The voice said, 'Well, go back and finish it.' I came back into my body.'" All the doctors and nurses were amazed that he didn't have any brain damage.

He will tell about his vision to anyone that will listen. He has told it as many times as God has given him opportunity to. He always tells them that they would go to their destination immediately and to be ready because Heaven is real, and so is Hell. Make sure you know which place you are going to end up at.

PERFORMERS

My husband, Floyd, and I went to minister to the residents at a local nursing home once a week. A lady named Grace sang for us with her beautiful voice. I always told her I felt she could sing with the best singers and I could hear angels singing with her. After knowing her a year, she died.

At home, I had a dream. I saw a huge amphitheater in Heaven. It looked like an amphitheater because it didn't have a roof to it. It was outside and was round in shape. Performers were on stage getting ready to sing.

I moved closer to see who they were. To my amazement, on the stage, I saw Grace, standing there with the gospel song writer, Dottie Rambo, Roy Rogers and Dale Evans and the Southern Gospel singing group, The Happy Goodmans.

Roy Rogers was a cowboy in the movies and had his own show in the early days of television. His real life wife, Dale Evans, was his co-star in many of these. Roy had a horse that was famous in his own right, Trigger. He performed in those TV shows and movies along with Roy and the horse could do many clever tricks. He was one of the best loved horses of all time. He was so beloved by both Roy and the public, that when Trigger died, Roy had him stuffed and placed him in their museum.

Roy said, "Dottie, do you know what I received when I arrived here?" He was looking at her and waiting for an answer.

"What was that, Roy?" she smilingly asked.

"A new horse", he chuckled.

Everyone in the audience was laughing. Grace was standing at the side getting ready to sing with them. It was good to see that Roy hadn't lost his sense of humor.

I don't believe that they saw me. No words were exchanged between us, but I wanted to shout with excitement, "Grace, I told you it would happen some day!" I woke up laughing and praising God.

Grace had a cousin at the same nursing home. I couldn't wait to tell her what I saw. She was so happy when I shared it with her, but sad that she couldn't be there with Grace.

Not My Will

I was helping a Pastor evangelize in the neighborhoods around the church. Suddenly, I felt I was having a heart attack. I was in so much pain, I could hardly breathe. Immediately, I rapidly went through the atmosphere and was standing in front of the bluest lake I had ever seen. It was so clear and appeared to be very deep. Two angels greeted me, one on each side.

I looked across the lake and I saw several people I knew, including my dad. I wanted to cross over. I wasn't in any pain.

"I want to come over there. Life is too hard on earth."

My dad told me I couldn't come there and I had to go back.

Do you think I wanted to hear that? No, I didn't!

I argued, "Let me talk to God about this. Why didn't he send Jesus Christ to talk to me?" I sat down, stubborn, not wanting to budge. "I'd rather sit here and wait until I can enter, instead of going back to earth." My dad was looking at me.

"God will show you something. Look." my dad said.

I looked to my right. High up, there were streams of light with the colors of pink, yellow, white, blue and green. It was like a rainbow, except not the normal rainbow colors. I listened and heard voices. It was the Pastor of the church that I was helping to evangelize for.

I knew that he was praying for me. "Lord, I need her ministry. Please send her back. Oh, God, I need help. Souls are lost", he was praying.

I looked at my dad and said, "What is that?"

"It's the prayers of saints going to God with their prayer requests."

I thought about what I had heard. Was my stubbornness more important than people not hearing the gospel and coming to know Jesus Christ? Was it worth it for me to enter now and go to my reward, but not know how many people I might have impacted for their eternity and where they would spend it? I could enter now and not fulfill my calling but the weight of all those people spending eternity in Hell because of my stubbornness was too much.

I cried. Then I said, "Not my will, but yours be done, Lord." The next thing I knew I was in my bed with the pain in my chest.

Early the next morning, the Pastor came to see me. "The Lord told me you were having a heart attack and dying. I told God I needed your ministry and not to take you. You need rest. You've been through a lot of tests. People don't understand you, but God does. You will be alright."

That was years ago. You wouldn't be reading this if I'd stayed there. A scripture came to my mind:

I Samuel 15:22 (KJV)

To obey is better than sacrifice.

If you are going through struggles, don't give up. You don't know what is in your future that God has for you. The greater the trials, the greater the blessings, is the tried and true saying. God told me that He always lets the devil go first with his messes, so that He can turn them around for miracles.

Another time when I visited Heaven and was allowed to go to the Throne Room, I saw the rainbow of lights to my right and God's left. I knew what it was, but I didn't hear any prayers at that time. I don't know if anyone else hears them, but I know God does. He hears every single prayer.

Peaceful Heaven

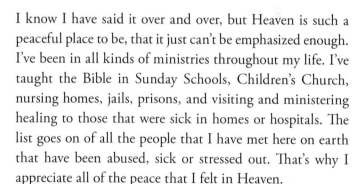

I know I have said it over and over, but Heaven is such a peaceful place to be, that it just can't be emphasized enough. I've been in all kinds of ministries throughout my life. I've taught the Bible in Sunday Schools, Children's Church, nursing homes, jails, prisons, and visiting and ministering healing to those that were sick in homes or hospitals. The list goes on of all the people that I have met here on earth that have been abused, sick or stressed out. That's why I appreciate all of the peace that I felt in Heaven.

Heaven is so well organized by God. It's a busy place with new people arriving all the time to be there permanently, or some just take a tour of that spectacular city so that we can write about it and show you that it is a real place and that you have a better place to go to once your time on earth is done.

Throughout this book I have referred many times to the term "saints". It's not because they were so perfect here on earth. It's because that is what God calls them, both on earth and in Heaven! The New Testament is filled with many examples of where Christians are called saints, and if you have read about the church at Corinth, you know that those people didn't have their acts together completely, by any means. It is because of their faith in Jesus Christ and for the sacrifice that He made for them on the cross with his very life, for their sins. They simply believed it and received Jesus Christ as their Savior. Don't think that you are disqualified from going to Heaven because you make mistakes.

You don't have to be afraid to die when God calls you home. Family and friends are summoned to meet you when you arrive. Angels will always take you. You don't go alone.

Worshipping God, playing games with one another, music, concerts, plays, dramas, comedies, and attending school are just some of the things that are done there. And of course, there is a time of rest, as I mentioned earlier. All I know is that God announces it's a time of rest, and everyone goes to their homes. It is all quiet. All activity stops, but I don't know for how long because I never did see a clock or anyone have a wrist watch on. Really, while I was there, I never thought about time. I wasn't told a lot of things, so I can only write what I saw, how I felt, or what I was told. God is always truthful.

My opinion could be wrong. I have tried not to add anything to my recollections of the visions that I have experienced. I have been asked many questions to which I don't know the answer to because it wasn't shown to me on my visits. I have read a lot of books by many people who have said that they visited Heaven. I cannot speak to their experiences, because many of them were vastly different than mine. They were taken to different places than I was. Heaven is an enormous place with lots to see and no one, but God, can experience it all. I'm hoping that once I am in Heaven for all eternity, I will have plenty of time to explore and will get to see it all.

So, some of our experiences are different and some of the things that we saw that were the same, like angels, appeared differently to us. I can't explain that. Each and every time I saw an angel there was always an extremely bright white light. No exceptions. But others don't relate their experience that way. I can only say that because we are all individuals, with different life experiences that help us to understand our world, perhaps God does the same thing when He shows us things in Heaven. Another way to put it is that I really love to plant and nurture flowers. God might show me flowers because I would really appreciate them. He might even explain something to me in a gardening term so that I would understand better. But, He couldn't do that to someone who has never seen a flower. He would use whatever life experiences that they have had to show them and explain things to them. These are just my opinions, mind you, but it is the only thing that explains to me why we do not all see the same things in the same ways.

So, although we write about Heaven so differently, we all agree on the love that is felt and that it is a real place.

People ask me why I've been allowed to see angels, Mary, the mother of Jesus, or have been in Heaven. I know beyond a shadow of a doubt that God wanted to show me these things to write this book.

Heaven is a real place. Almighty God is alive and He is Holy. Eternity is forever. God wants you to go to Heaven to be with Him for all of time. It is a fun place with many things to do; a perfect place full of love. All of your heart's desires are fulfilled there.

John 3:16 (KJV)

> For God so loved the world that He gave His only begotten Son, that whosoever believeth in Him should not perish, but have everlasting life.

In Revelation, the 21st chapter, it tells us a lot about Heaven. The devil goes before God in Heaven to accuse the saints on earth now. But the new Heaven and Earth, the devil will never see it.

I was told by God once that every time the devil goes before God to get permission to attack or test someone, he goes away more angry, because he desires to have all the control that God does. It wasn't God's intention for the devil to be destroyed. The devil destroyed himself. God knew it ahead of time, but because He is just and believes in free-will, He allowed the devil to choose.

The devil is a liar. He still believes he will be able to overthrow God at the Battle of Armageddon and all of God's people. The devil is working very hard to destroy God's people now. We need to warn people to WAKE UP!

I want to encourage everyone to live your Christianity and not be hypocritical. Others are watching you. A lot of churches these days are teaching a "feel good" gospel and not teaching the whole Word of God. God hasn't changed. He is still a Holy God that is against sin. And He's still a God who wants what is best for you. And he still wants to talk to you and show you great and marvelous truths. Mostly, that happens by reading His love letter to us, the Bible. If you know the Word, then you cannot be deceived. To know the truth will set you free.

What God Said

In one of the visions that I related earlier, (see the chapter "Schooling") when I was having a conversation with God about things, here is the rest of the talk that we had that day.

I did not see God when we talked, but I heard his voice as we talked. I asked him if he was hurt about anything because I saw a lot of suffering while I was on earth.

"The saddest day for me will be the final judgment when I have to tell people to depart from me, that I don't know them. They think they can accept my son and keep on living in their sins. I gave my only son to die for their sins. I gave them my Word. They can't serve two masters. Be clean, be holy and love one another. Give me first place in their hearts. My Word doesn't change. People are changing it more and more. I am happy with the ones that love me and serve me."

Further reading:

John 3:15	Luke 13:15
John 1:1	Luke 16:13
John 13:15	I Peter 1:15

FREQUENTLY ASKED QUESTIONS

People ask me questions of all kinds once they know that I've seen Heaven. By all means, I am no authority on it. I don't believe I saw it all. There's a lot more I don't know and haven't seen. Below are some questions that I have been asked by others, and God answered either verbally or by showing me in the visions He gave me. I call these my Frequently Asked Questions!

Q: Is everyone's robe the same?

A: The robes of white are all different. The details of each robe depend on the work you do for me and my son, Jesus.

Q: What changes do our spirits have?

A: There are no scars, tattoos, paintings or body-piercings.

Q: What about your hair?

A: You can keep it the length you want. It will be kept that way for you because it is part of your reward.

Q: Will men have beards?

A: If they want them. No need for them to cut them. Again, they will be kept that way for them. No one has to shave, because their bodies are different than on earth.

Q: Will my family know me?

A: Christians that died and went to Heaven, when you get there, they will know you and you will know them.

Q: What size are you after death?

A: From the time of the death on earth you are immediately in full health and perfect size because you are a spirit. You are recognized. No exercise or dieting is needed. No allergies. Everyone can eat the same fruits in Heaven.

Q: What about babies and children?

A: They are healthy and will be growing, but never get old. No one will look their age.

Q: Do you eat in Heaven?

A: Yes. Fruits. No meat. The Word of God is the meat. It's a process when you eat—it goes. No bathrooms. You don't have blood or bones there. You are a spirit; perfect!

Q: What language do you speak?

A: All one language. You will know it when you get there.

Q: What will our names be?

A: The same as they were on earth until after the final Judgment.

Q: What do they talk about?

A: Sightseeing, games, families, how good God is, thanking Christ for saving them. Whatever their talents are; school and what you learned. Asking if family, friends, and neighbors will be saved.

Q: What about school?

A: The angels teach the Word of God. They have been trained by me. They will teach you one thing per lesson. Once you learn it, you won't forget it. There are so many details to one page of the Bible. There is so much about the Bible to learn that you will be learning through all of eternity, but still will never know all that I know.

Q: What do you do?

A: Read, play, worship, rest, write, make things, talk, enjoy everything. Love is everywhere, in everyone. You are a servant, therefore, you are asking fellow saints, "What can I do for you?" and "Can I help you?"

Q: What about fishing?

A: Not anything that causes blood or death. You don't eat fish here.

Q: Is there a miniature golf course?

A: The real thing is taught here.

Q: What recreation is there?

A: Swimming, tennis, boating, golf, plays, writing, horseback riding, ball games, picnics, visiting, meeting saints. Flowers, drawing, craft. There are many, many things to do. There are games here that you don't have on earth.

Q: Are there any animals?

A: Yes. Dogs, cats, birds, horses, dolphins, ostriches, flamingoes, doves and lions. There are no wild animals in Heaven because animals are free to walk around. There are no cages. I'm sure there are more, but I can only mention the animals that I saw. They were always clean and well.

Q: Where do you live?

A: If you have loved ones that you got along with on earth, you could live with them. You are also grouped by your learning and doing of the Word. You are the light of the world, and your light shines in Heaven.

Q: What about Christians that are saved but not fully delivered?

A: For people that did really bad things and feel guilty about it, that weren't delivered but do accept Christ, and they die and go to Heaven, they will stay in a place I have prepared for them. It is just inside the city. Angels or other saints will counsel them. Their unworthiness will leave when they realize the blood of Jesus Christ made them worthy. If they have relatives from earth in Heaven, they are summoned to talk to them. Forgiveness is in a greater measure. They have to accept the forgiveness before they can feel all the love.

Q: Will everyone meet each other in Heaven?

A: Eternity is forever, so there will be plenty of time to meet everyone. There is a desire to meet everyone because you know you are all family.

Q: Will you see God, Jesus Christ and the Holy Spirit?

A: The brightness of God is hard for anyone to "see" the fullness of God. You can see Jesus Christ. The Holy Spirit is a presence you can feel, not see. (Remember I haven't died yet. My spirit could see clearer.)

I was also told:

That there are flower gardens to look at but no vegetable gardens.

The people from Africa that wore metal and bone body piercings will not wear them in Heaven.

There will be no painted faces, such as the Indians wore (war paint). They do wear very colorful robes, white with colors. They live close to the sea. They love the water. They have colorful canoes that are white with Indian designs on them.

The Eskimos live in a place around the mountains. It has snow, but it isn't cold there.

A huge lake is there that is crystal clear blue water. You can see in it, but you can't see to the bottom of it.

In Closing

I knew when I was shown these things and God told me to write about my experiences, that there would be many who would believe and many more who would not. I wasn't told to convince people, but only to write about what I'd seen or tell what He told me to tell. All I can say is that you should pray about it.

I hope that by sharing these glimpses of Heaven will encourage you. Perhaps it will help you heal from pain, suffering and the loss of loved ones. Just remember that we never walk alone. He is always with us.

Hope to see you over there!

Carol

Printed in the United States
By Bookmasters